The Amazing History of Transportation

MACHINES IN MOTION

ILLUSTRATED BY

TOM JACKSON  CHRIS MOULD

BLOOMSBURY
CHILDREN'S BOOKS
NEW YORK LONDON OXFORD NEW DELHI SYDNEY

CONTENTS

Introduction 3

Trains 4

Overground &
Underground 8

Ships 12

More Ships 16

Cars 20

More Cars 24

Balloons 28

Bikes 32

Airplanes 36

Tanks 40

Helicopters 44

Working Vehicles 48

Submarines 52

Rockets 56

Spacecraft 60

INTRODUCTION

Every day, all over the world, people are busy traveling—making short hops or long voyages, moving slowly and steadily, or racing along at super-fast speeds. People travel in cars, trains, planes, ships, and on bikes—and some people even blast off in rockets!

From the earliest times, people have used technology to invent efficient and imaginative ways of getting around. Did you know the first boats were built 7,000 years ago, the ancient Greeks built something very similar to a railway, and the Chinese made the first rockets in the 7th century BCE?

Where would we be without the wheel? Luckily, we don't need to know the answer to this, because wheels have been used to help us whiz around quickly and smoothly for thousands of years. It's not the only incredible transport invention, though—steam power, gasoline engines, propellers, and spacecraft are just some of the inventions that have made journeys longer, faster, and more amazing.

In this book, you can make your own amazing journeys by exploring timelines packed with trains, planes, cars, helicopters, and more, and by discovering the people and stories behind the machines that keep the world moving.

All aboard!

TRAINS

Trains were the first form of on-land mass transportation; they could carry hundreds of passengers long before cars or buses were invented. Trains work so well because the rails on the train track give the wheels a smooth place to roll over, so even huge trains can go really fast. Today, trains are still the longest wheeled vehicles there are. The longest ones stretch more than four miles and are found whizzing through Australia.

Wagonways

1781 Steam power
Thomas Savery (c. 1650–1715) invented the first steam engine in 1698, but the early designs were weak and often broke apart. In 1781, James Watt (1736–1819), a Scottish engineer, redesigned the steam engine to make it much more powerful. Watt's engines could also be made small enough to power a vehicle—a train perhaps?

1500s Wagonways
The first railways were built underground by miners in Germany and around central Europe. They needed an easy way to shift the coal, metal ore, and rock they dug up, so they invented the wagonway. It didn't look much like a railway as we know it, though—the tracks were made of logs or thick wooden planks and the carts and wagons ran over the top.

The mine carts were very heavy and small, but tough horses or mules (also called pit ponies) were brought in to pull them. One of the last pit ponies to work in Great Britain was named Tony. He died in 2011 aged 40 years old. That's very old for a horse—they really were tough!

James Watt

Steam engine

1804 Steam locomotives
Richard Trevithick (1771–1833), a mining engineer from Cornwall, England, built a series of steam-powered locomotives. These mighty machines were so heavy that they cracked the wooden rails they rolled along. Luckily, Trevithick worked for an ironworks and so he began using iron and other strong metals to build rails that his trains could roll along.

In 1808, Trevithick took his best steam engine, which he named the Catch Me Who Can, to London. He built a circular railway track for it to run on and charged people to take a ride on his "Steam Circus." It reached a maximum speed of 12 miles per hour, and riders were thrilled by the high-speed ride!

Richard Trevithick

Catch Me Who Can

1825–1830 Public transportation
Railways were built at mines and quarries to haul heavy loads. British engineer George Stephenson (1781–1848) built one of the largest mining railways between Stockton and Darlington in England. Passengers could also travel on the railway—but only if they were pulled along by a horse. At the time, people thought that the speed of a steam engine would be too fast for the body to withstand! Stephenson went on to build the first intercity passenger railway, which ran for 40 miles between Liverpool and Manchester.

Stockton to Darlington railway

George Stephenson

Stephenson's Rocket

1829 Stephenson's Rocket

In 1829, a competition was held to find the best steam-engine design. Ten locomotives were entered but only five made it to the starting line, and only one locomotive completed the short course. It was the Rocket, and its designer was . . . George Stephenson.

1869 US transcontinental railroad

During the American Civil War (1861–1865) it was almost impossible to connect the east and west coasts of the United States. Two of the biggest rail companies raced to build a track across the continent. One company started to build a track in the east and the other started to build in the west.

In 1869, after six years of work, the two tracks met in Utah and the final rail was hammered into place with a golden nail. The 1,907-mile transcontinental railroad was open. A journey from New York to San Francisco now took just six days—it took six months before!

1912 Diesel

After cars were invented in 1885, several inventors tried to build trains that used the same gas-powered engines. But they were not powerful enough. In 1893, Rudolf Diesel (1858–1913) invented a tougher engine that burned a thick, greasy fuel—diesel! The first diesel-powered trains ran in Switzerland in 1912. If you see a noisy and smelly train engine today, it is a diesel one.

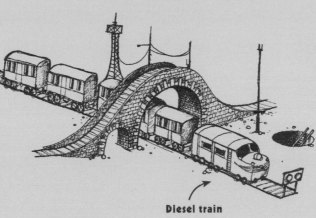

Diesel train

1981 TGV

Today, most passenger trains are powered by electric motors. The electricity supply comes from wires that run overhead above the track or along a third rail on the track. In France, these trains are called TGVs—this is short for "*train à grande vitesse*," which means "high-speed train" in French. They can travel over 350 miles per hour, which is twice as fast as a jumbo jet during take-off! In Japan, these high-speed engine trains are called bullet trains.

The Shanghai Maglev

2004 Shanghai Maglev

The fastest trains of all do not have engines or normal tracks. They float, or levitate, using powerful magnets. These trains are called maglevs. The fastest passenger-carrying maglev today connects Shanghai, China, to Pudong International Airport. The 20-mile journey takes just eight minutes! (This journey would take a normal train about four times as long.) Inventors are still experimenting with new maglevs. There is a Japanese train that goes faster than 370 miles per hour. That is half the speed of sound!

US transcontinental railroad

OVERGROUND & UNDERGROUND

Hohensalzburg Castle

1515 CE
Funicular railway

600 BCE
The Diolkos

1863
The Metropolitan
Railway

600 BCE
The Diolkos is built in
Corinth, ancient Greece

1515 CE
The first funicular railway is
opened at Hohensalzburg
Castle in Salzburg, Austria

1644
Adam Wybe invents the
cable car in Gdansk, Poland

OVERGROUND & UNDERGROUND

High-speed trains need flat and straight railways to travel over. But the Earth is not flat or straight; it's full of tall mountains, twisting rivers, and deep oceans. Luckily, engineers have figured out a way of getting people over—or perhaps under—these obstacles. There's no stopping us now!

600 BCE Diolkos

Corinth, a city in ancient Greece, lay on a narrow strip of land between two seas. To sail from one side to the other involved a long and dangerous sea journey all the way around Greece. It would be much quicker to move the ships overland. So that's exactly what the ancient Greeks did. The ships were hauled out of the water and onto carts, which ran along grooves cut into the rocky ground. The grooved trackway was called the Diolkos.

1515 CE Funicular

Many castles in Austria were built on top of mountains. The only way to reach them was up long, winding roads that zigzagged up the slopes. In 1515, a new, faster, and less tiring route was created at Hohensalzburg Castle in Salzburg. It was a funicular, which is a cross between a train carriage and an elevator. A track was bolted to the steep, rocky mountainside beneath the castle. Goods were hauled straight up inside a small carriage that ran along the track but was pulled by a rope. To get down again, the carriage was lowered slowly back down the track.

Funicular railway

Diolkos

1644 Cable car

Dutch engineer Adam Wybe (1584–1653) was asked to build new walls and castles around Gdansk, Poland. To do so, he collected building materials from Bishop's Mountain, which was on the other side of the river from the castle. To carry the materials across the water, Wybe built a system of cables and baskets supported on tall towers. There were 120 baskets that rotated on a loop: half went across the water empty as the other half came back full. Wybe had invented the cable car.

In 1873, a different system of cable car opened in San Francisco, California, designed by British inventor Andrew Hallidie (1836–1900). Instead of hanging from a moving cable, the cable cars grabbed hold of a cable that ran under the street—this hauled passengers up and over the city's steep hills.

Cable car

Monorail

1825 Monorail

A monorail is a train track that has just one rail, not two. Monorails can be built in crowded cities where there is no room for an ordinary railway, because their tracks can sweep high above the ground.

1994 Channel Tunnel

Some stretches of water are too wide and too deep for a bridge, so the only thing to do is build a tunnel underneath. In 1988, work started on a rail tunnel under the seabed of the English Channel, creating the first dry route between Britain and France for 180,000 years. It was completed in 1994.

The Channel Tunnel is the longest undersea tunnel in the world; it is 31 miles long and about 250 feet below sea level. Every day, 500 trains thunder through the tunnels at 99 miles per hour.

1863 Underground

Today, there are about 160 underground railways in 55 countries that take travelers all around crowded cities. Every city has a different name or nickname for their underground: in New York it's the subway, in Berlin it's the U-Bahn, in Paris it's the Metro, and in London it's the Tube.

Open since 1863, the London Undergound is the oldest underground railway. At first, the trains were steam-powered and the tunnels had holes in the roof so the smoke from the engines could get out. This system was soon copied all over the world.

Underground

1994
Channel Tunnel

985
A longship sinks in Hedeby harbor in Denmark. It is discovered there in 1953

1492
Christopher Columbus sails to America in an early design of a carrack called the *Santa María*

1783
Pyroscaphe, the first steamboat, is launched on the River Saône, France

1843
SS Great Britain, the largest iron ship of its time, is built by the English engineer Isambard Kingdom Brunel

SHIPS

Boats are the oldest form of transportation. As long as 40,000 years ago, people sailed all the way from Africa to Australia and stopped off in Asia along the way. Some boats were built to make short voyages along the coast, but longer journeys that went far out to sea required bigger and faster ships—and many new inventions. All aboard!

Neptune

8040 BCE Dugout canoe

The first boats were built from fallen logs that were hollowed out. They were called dugout canoes and they were used by ancient sailors all over the world. A canoe made from a really big tree could carry as many as 100 people!

Dugout canoe

Longship

1000s CE Longship

Viking longships were built to sail across rough seas. They voyaged across the Atlantic Ocean looking for new places for the Vikings to live—or at least attack! Unlike most ships, the front of a longship was the same shape as the back. This meant the ships could easily change direction while avoiding collisions with icebergs.

5000 BCE Reed boats

The people of Mesopotamia were also masters at building riverboats. Instead of using wood, these boats were made from bundles of reeds that were woven and lashed together.

Reed boat

750 BCE Ancient Greek galley

Galleys are made of wood and are powered by lots of long oars. The ancient Greeks built galleys with more decks so that they could fit more oarsmen. Traveling at speeds of up to 16 miles per hour, galleys were the fastest ships afloat! Ancient Greek galleys had bronze battering rams that stuck out of their bows. The sharp ram was hidden under the water so the enemy only knew it was there after it had ripped a hole in their boat! The Romans also built great fleets of galleys.

Roman galley

Viking

Carrack →

1500s Carrack

The carrack was built so European traders could carry cargo over long distances across oceans. Carracks were also well equipped for sea battles. Cannons poked out of little doors, or ports, in the hull. In 1519, five carracks with 237 crew left Portugal to sail around the world for the first time. In 1522, only one ship with 14 of those original crew members (and four new ones) made it home again—completing the first round-the-world voyage.

1783 Steamboat

The steamboat was the first boat to be powered by an engine instead of by sails or oars. The steam engine was used to drive a paddlewheel. The inventor was Claude-François-Dorothée, marquis de Jouffroy d'Abbans (1751–1832). Luckily, his riverboat had a simpler name than he did: *Pyroscaphe*.

1843 Ocean liner

In 1843, a new type of ship was built—the ocean liner. It was made entirely of iron and was powered by steam engines that turned a propeller. The first ocean liner was the *SS Great Britain*, designed by the ingenious mechanical and civil engineer Isambard Kingdom Brunel (1806–1859). It was the largest ship of its time, with enough cargo space for 200 elephants! For many years it sailed across the Atlantic and then later took people to live in Australia. On a voyage to Melbourne in 1861, the *SS Great Britain* carried one cow, 36 sheep, 96 goats, 1,114 chickens, 143 sailors, and 544 passengers—including the English cricket team heading to play Australia for the first time. England won!

Isambard Kingdom Brunel →

Steamboat →

SS Great Britain →

MORE SHIPS

1897
Turbinia

1906
HMS
Dreadnought

Ship ahoy!

1912
The *Titanic*

1959
SR.N1
hovercraft

2013
USS *Zumwalt*

2017
IDEC SPORT
trimaran

1897
Charles Parsons sails the
Turbinia into the middle
of a naval display

1906
HMS *Dreadnought*
is launched, the first
high-speed battleship

1912
The *Titanic* ocean liner goes
down in the Atlantic Ocean

1914
The Panama Canal
opens

1959
The first hovercraft,
SR.N1, sails across the
English Channel

1914
The Panama Canal

1961
USS Enterprise

1979
Seawise Giant

1961
The first nuclear-powered aircraft carrier, USS *Enterprise*, takes to the seas

1979
The *Seawise Giant* is the longest and heaviest ship ever built

2013
Futuristic battleship USS *Zumwalt* is launched

2017
The IDEC SPORT trimaran sets a new record for sailing around the world

MORE SHIPS

Ships are the biggest vehicles there are. Huge tankers and gigantic cargo ships can be up to four times as long as a soccer field. Immense aircraft carriers work like floating airports, with a runway for fast jets to whiz down. All ships float, of course, but there are some vessels that float on air instead of water, and the latest stealth ships seem to disappear into thin air as well!

The Panama Canal →

1890 Turbine engine

Giant iron ships used huge steam engines that burned through tons of coal to cross the sea. In the 1890s, Charles Parsons (1854–1931) invented a new engine called a turbine. It used a blast of hot steam to spin a fan (that's the turbine) that made the propeller go around. Parsons thought turbine engines were perfect for battleships, but the Royal Navy disagreed.

In 1897, the navy's best ships sailed to Portsmouth to put on a show. Parsons ruined the show by sailing his high-speed turbine-powered boat, *Turbinia*, up and down in front of the admirals. The admirals sent their fastest ships to catch him, but none of them were fast enough. After that, all new battleships were fitted with Parsons's turbines!

1906 *Dreadnought*

The first turbine-powered battleship was called HMS *Dreadnought*. It could go 24 miles per hour at full speed. The mighty HMS *Dreadnought* was covered in heavy metal armor up to 11 inches thick! This protected the ship from torpedoes and bombs—it could dread nothing. However, HMS *Dreadnought* never went into battle. The biggest battleship clash ever was in 1916, when 250 ships from Britain and Germany met near Jutland, Denmark. Unfortunately, the *Dreadnought* was in dock being given a tune-up while the World War I battle was fought.

1912 *Titanic*

In April 1912, an enormous luxury ocean liner called the *Titanic* set sail for New York, USA, from Southampton, England. It was big enough to carry 2,200 passengers and crew and was built so it could never sink. The hull was divided into watertight sections: even if four of them filled up with water, the ship would still float. After three days at sea the *Titanic* hit an iceberg. Not four, but five of the hull sections were flooded. The *Titanic* sank! About 1,500 people drowned in the icy water because the "unsinkable" ship did not have enough lifeboats for everyone on board.

The Titanic ↓

1914 Panama Canal

Until 1914 the only way to travel from New York to San Francisco by sea was by going all the way around South America. But then the Panama Canal opened. The 110-foot-wide canal ran for 48 miles. It shortened a ship's journey by more than 9,000 miles! Digging the canal was a big job. It took ten years to build, and the rock and earth that were dug out were enough to cover the whole island of Manhattan, New York, in a layer 12 feet deep.

To get through the Panama Canal you need a Panamax ship. Ships that are bigger than this will not fit into the 12 locks along the canal. The ships do not use their own engines in the locks. "Mules," super-strong electric train engines that run along tracks beside the canal, haul them into the locks.

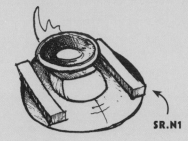

SR.N1

1959 Hovercraft

In 1959, Christopher Cockerell (1910–1999), a British engineer, designed a completely new type of ship, the hovercraft. Hovercraft run over water on a cushion of air. Cockerell combined boat and aircraft technology. Big fans push air under the boat, filling a big rubber bag, and make the craft hover above the water. Hovercraft are pushed forward by a propeller at the back and are steered by rudders similar to those on an airplane tail.

Unlike other ships, hovercraft can travel on land as well—as long as the surface is flat. However, they are hard to control because they do not have brakes and will just keep sliding across the surface.

1979 *Seawise Giant*

The longest and heaviest ship ever built was the *Seawise Giant*. This oil tanker was 1500 feet long. The *Seawise Giant*'s job was to carry oil, and when it was fully loaded it weighed 724,200 tons (that is about the same as 3,600 blue whales). Everything about the *Seawise Giant* was huge—even its anchor weighed the same as ten elephants.

However, big is not always best. The ship was too large to sail in shallow seas. In the end, the *Seawise Giant* was converted into an oil storage vessel and was eventually broken up in 2010.

Seawise Giant

2013 USS *Zumwalt*

The USS *Zumwalt* is a futuristic battleship. With its smooth sides and pointed bow, the USS *Zumwalt* is a stealth vessel. Normally, radar waves can bounce off big ships and make an echo that can be picked up by other battleships. However, the USS *Zumwalt*'s design makes only a small echo on a radar screen—so small that this 610-foot battleship could be mistaken for an 80-foot fishing boat. That sounds confusing, and it is meant to be—the idea is that the enemy cannot see it coming.

USS *Zumwalt*

2017 IDEC SPORT trimaran

The quickest way to sail around the world is by using a sail-powered yacht. It can keep going when other ships have run out of fuel. In 2017, a crew of six aboard the IDEC SPORT trimaran set a new around-the-world record, taking 40 days, 23 hours, and 30 minutes. Most of the journey was through the Southern Ocean near Antarctica, where the winds are very strong and it is very cold. A trimaran yacht has three separate hulls with wide gaps in between. It can move much faster than other ships because big waves that slow down bigger ships can roll under the racing yacht between its hulls.

USS *Enterprise*

1961 Supercarrier

The first aircraft carriers were built after World War I, and they gradually became the most powerful vessels afloat. In 1961, the first supercarrier, USS *Enterprise*, was launched. It was a floating airport and it could travel across water at 38 miles per hour. On the deck was a 111-foot runway that was used by 90 aircraft.

Supercarriers are powered by nuclear reactors. The heat from the reactors makes steam to power the turbines. The fuel supply lasts for 20 years, so the ships only come back to port to swap crew and restock on food supplies.

IDEC SPORT trimaran

CARS

Where would we be without the wheel? Not very far away, that's where. Some say that the wheel is the most important invention in human history. It has a long story, which begins in a rather unusual way.

Coach →

Pottery wheel →

3500s BCE Wheel

The first wheel was actually created to make pottery. Around 6,500 years ago, a clever potter in the Middle East started making bowls by spinning clay on a round wooden board. Another 300 years later, people started spinning boards on top of a pole, or axle. Does this sound familiar? The wheel had been invented.

3300s BCE Cart

The first vehicles with wheels were built around 5,300 years ago, probably in Mesopotamia. Box-shaped carts were balanced on an axle that had a wheel at each end. The wheels were made of planks of wood nailed together. For the cart to go in a straight line, all the wheels needed to be the same size.

Cart ↓

1700s BCE Chariot

Early war wagons were heavy and not very fast or easy to steer. But around 3,700 years ago, an army of invaders called the Hyksos from Central Asia used a force of 3,500 horse-drawn chariots to defeat the mighty ancient Egyptian army. The chariots could go much faster than war wagons because they had wheels made with spokes. (Spokes are supports that connect the center of the wheel to the rim.) Spoked wheels are much lighter than solid wooden wheels and can be made larger, which means they travel further with every roll. The Egyptians eventually learned how to build them and kicked the Hyksos out!

Chariots →

1470s CE Coach

Wagons and chariots were uncomfortable—you could feel every rock and imperfection in the road. So, cartwrights in northern Hungary designed a cart that sat on springs that could absorb the shock of big bumps in the road. This made journeys much smoother and more comfortable. This system is called a suspension. Suspension was invented in a place called Kocs (pronounced "kotch") and the "carts of Kocs" became popular all over the world. Today we know a "cart of Kocs" as a "coach."

Steam carriage →

1769 Steam carriage

In 1769, French inventor Nicolas-Joseph Cugnot (1725–1804) invented a vehicle that was propelled by an engine instead of horses—the first car! The huge three-wheeled steam carriage was designed to carry heavy cannons, but it was not a great success. It had a top speed of 2.5 miles per hour and it ran out of fuel in just 15 minutes. On its first drive, it ran out of control (slowly) and crashed into a wall—the first car accident!

1885 Benz Patent-Motorwagen

Many people tried to build cars, but it usually went dangerously wrong. Finally, German inventor Karl Benz (1844–1929) built a car that actually worked. It was called the Benz Patent-Motorwagen; it had three wheels and was powered by a small gasoline engine. Karl's wife and business partner, Bertha Benz (1849–1944), made it famous when she took it on the world's first long-distance road trip in 1888. Karl Benz developed many new designs of car—he soon added a fourth wheel, a steering wheel, and headlights. In 1901, Emil Jellinek (1853–1918) bought the Benz Company. He added his daughter's name to it, creating the world-famous company name Mercedes-Benz.

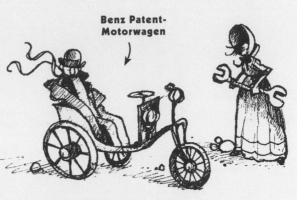

Benz Patent-Motorwagen

1908 Ford Model T

To begin with, every car was built by hand. Henry Ford (1863–1947), an American businessman, changed all that. In 1908 he designed a car called the Model T that could be made very quickly in his factory. All the parts were made separately and then joined together. The production line took 93 minutes to assemble one car in 84 steps. A new car came out the other end every three minutes! By 1920, nearly half of all the cars in the world were Ford Model Ts. When production stopped in 1927, there were 15 million of them zooming around the roads. Ford cars were cheap enough for ordinary people to buy. The Car Age had arrived.

Hippomobile

1863 Hippomobile

A steam engine is an external combustion engine—the power comes from hot steam that is burned outside the engine and then used to push on pistons that are sealed inside cylinders. In 1860, the Belgian-French engineer Étienne Lenoir (1822–1900) invented an internal combustion engine where the gas was burned *inside* the cylinders. It was a more efficient design than the steam engine. In 1863, Lenoir used his engine to power a little carriage called the Hippomobile. He went for a drive in the Hippomobile, heading out of Paris, France. It took 90 minutes to reach the edge of the city, a distance of seven miles. He could almost have walked it in that time!

Model T Ford

MORE CARS

1947 Ferrari

1911 Monte Carlo rally

2016 Electric cars

2010 Bugatti Veyron Super Sport

Charger

1997 Thrust SSC

Wing Commander Andy Green

1911
The first Monte Carlo rally is held

1947
The first Ferrari sports cars are built

1950
The first Formula 1 Grand Prix is held in Silverstone, England

1963
Drag racers begin using top fuel

1950
Formula 1 car

1975
Bigfoot
monster truck

1963
Drag racers

1975
The first monster truck,
nown as Bigfoot, is built

1997
Thrust SSC becomes
the first car to break
the sound barrier

2010
The Bugatti Veyron
Super Sport becomes
the fastest car designed
to drive on public roads

2016
Electric cars made
by Tesla are built
with an autopilot

MORE CARS

Today there are more than a billion cars in the world. Cars have changed a lot over the last century. Most cars are still just a way to help us get around—to school, to the store, to work, or to visit friends and relatives. However, since the beginning of car technology, drivers have wanted to go faster and faster!

1911 Sports cars

Sports cars are designed to be fast, comfortable, and above all fun to drive. The first sports cars were not so comfortable, but they were actually used in a sport—a new competition known as a "rally." The first Monte Carlo rally was held in 1911. Twenty-three cars set off from all over Europe, hoping to be the first to reach Monte Carlo, Monaco. The cars were called "roadsters;" they had two seats and were built for long-distance journeys. The cars used in the Monte Carlo rally were built for racing on normal roads. The cars almost always broke the speed limit, which was very dangerous. The winner of the rally was not the first driver to reach Monte Carlo, but the car that crossed the line in the most style (and still in one piece). Even today, the best sports cars have to look really good as well as go really fast.

Monte Carlo rally

1950 Formula 1 Grand Prix

In 1950, a new style of car race appeared: the Formula 1 Grand Prix. F-1 cars were only driven on tracks specially built for racing. They only have one seat and they are driven by some of the best drivers in the world. F-1 racers can go so fast—about three times faster than a regular car can drive—that they are at risk of taking off like an aircraft! The trick to keeping them safely on the ground is to add a wing to the back of the car. That sounds like it would make the problem worse, but the wing is attached upside down. This means that, instead of lifting the vehicle into the air, it pushes it firmly down to the ground.

Formula 1 racer

Drag racers

1963 Drag racing

In a drag race, the aim is for the drivers to accelerate forward in a straight line as fast as possible. In 1963, it became legal for dragsters—long cars with huge engines—to use a top fuel, a highly explosive liquid called nitromethane, or "nitro." It burns eight times faster than the fuel in a normal car—meaning the dragster can reach more than 300 miles per hour in less than four seconds. Drag races are short but exciting!

2020 Electric cars

In the future, cars will not need to fill up with fuel; they will be powered by electric motors supplied by giant batteries. Today's electric cars can drive just as fast as gasoline-powered cars, but their batteries need regular recharging. In the future, there will be better batteries that can power cars for long journeys. Driving will be easier than ever before because a computer will control the car while you sit back and enjoy the view. The car will use cameras, radars, and light-beam systems to steer and watch out for other cars on the road.

Electric cars

Thrust SSC

1997 Thrust SSC

The Thrust Super Sonic Car is the fastest car of all time. It is powered by two jet engines taken from a fighter plane! The Thrust SSC's driver is fighter pilot Wing Commander Andy Green from England. In 1997, the Thrust SSC became the first and only car to break the sound barrier. Driving on a long, straight course in the Nevada desert, it reached an incredible 763 miles per hour and created a loud thunderclap as it punched through the sound barrier. (Usually only rockets and fighter jets can make that noise!)

BALLOONS

2016
Airlander 10

1783
The first
hot-air
balloon

1783
The first hot-air
balloon is invented
by the Montgolfier
brothers in France

1783
Jacques Charles invents
the first hydrogen
balloon in France

1852
Henri Giffard invents
the first airship, the
dirigible, in France

1900
Count Ferdinand von
Zeppelin invents the
zeppelin airship in
Germany

1960
Echo 1 balloon satellite
is launched into space
from the USA

1852
Dirigible

1703
Hydrogen
balloon

1999
Breitling
Orbiter

2012
Felix
Baumgartner

1960
Echo 1
satellite

1900
Zeppelin

The
Hindenburg

1999
Breitling Orbiter becomes the first balloon to fly around the world without stopping

2012
Felix Baumgartner jumps from a height of 24 miles and becomes the first person to skydive faster than the speed of sound

2016
The Airlander 10, the world's biggest balloon, is built in the UK

BALLOONS

Believe it or not, balloons were actually invented before cars and trains. They float up into the air in the same way that air bubbles rise in water. Up, up, and away!

1783 Hot-air balloon

The first hot-air balloon was built in France by the Montgolfier brothers (Joseph-Michel, 1740–1810, and Jacques-Étienne, 1745–1799), two makers of paper. The balloon was constructed from thin paper and silk covered in varnish to prevent it from catching fire. The first aviators to board a hot-air balloon were a duck, a chicken, and a sheep. The sheep was chosen because people thought its body would react similarly to humans', and the brothers wanted to see if it would be hurt by the flight. The duck could already fly quite high so it should have been fine if anything went wrong—and the fluttering chicken was somewhere in between the other passengers. A few months later, two brave Frenchmen became the first humans to fly. They traveled in a huge Montgolfier balloon that was twice as tall as a house. A wood fire hung underneath the balloon in an iron cage to keep it aloft. In the end the fire began to burn the balloon, but luckily they managed to land safely.

1783 Hydrogen balloon

Eleven days after the Montgolfiers' famous balloon flight, another French inventor, Jacques Charles (1746–1823), launched a different kind of balloon. His was filled with hydrogen gas, which is lighter than air but also highly explosive. Charles's balloon shot up nearly two miles into the air and had to make an emergency landing almost immediately. Charles had given his balloon a test run, but it blew away too fast and landed in a distant field. Unfortunately, it was attacked by terrified farmers who had never seen anything that could fly before.

1852 Dirigible

Most balloons cannot be steered—they just go wherever the wind blows them. Henri Giffard (1825–1882) built the first steerable balloon, which he called a dirigible. It was filled with hydrogen and powered by a steam engine that spun a propeller. It could reach 6 miles per hour, as long as there was no wind. The dirigible became better known as the airship.

Hydrogen balloon

1900 Zeppelin

Count Ferdinand von Zeppelin (1838–1917), a German soldier, invented an airship with a lightweight metal frame. Many small hydrogen balloons were enclosed inside the frame, which meant he could make the aircraft really huge. These aircraft became known as zeppelins. They were the largest flying machines around. The *Graf Zeppelin* was three times longer than a jumbo jet and only slightly smaller than the *Titanic* ocean liner!

Zeppelin

The first hot-air balloon

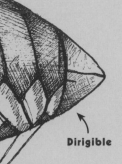

Dirigible

1931 Flying aircraft carrier

The United States Navy built the USS *Akron*, the first flying aircraft carrier. It carried a fleet of Sparrowhawks (little propeller-powered fighter planes). The fighters were dropped from the *Akron*, and the skilled pilots would reattach them to the USS *Akron* again in mid-air. Sadly, in 1933, It crashed, killing 73 people.

Hindenburg

1937 *Hindenburg*

Large passenger cabins were added to zeppelins and they began making long journeys. They took two or three days to fly across the Atlantic Ocean, and one even circled the globe in less than a month! However, in 1937, diaster struck when the hydrogen inside the *Hindenburg* passenger zeppelin exploded as it landed and killed 35 people. No one flew in zeppelins after that.

1960 Project Echo

The first communication satellite was a metal balloon launched into space by a rocket. It was folded up so it was very small for the launch, and once it was in orbit the balloon was pumped up with gases. Used for bouncing radio messages around the world, it was like a giant shiny space mirror.

Echo 1

Felix Baumgartner

1999 Breitling Orbiter

The huge helium-filled Breitling Orbiter 3 was the first balloon to fly all the way around the world without landing. The balloon carried two passengers and the flight took nearly 20 days.

2012 Supersonic skydiver

Felix Baumgartner used a helium balloon called the Red Bull Stratos to fly to a height of 24 miles—and then he jumped out! He fell for more than four minutes and became the first person to skydive faster than the speed of sound. That is six times faster than a regular skydiver!

Red Bull Stratos

Breitling Orbiter

BIKES

Wheeeee! Where will these running machines lead?

1817 Dandy horse

Get pedaling and you can power your own transport machine!

Karl von Drais (1785–1851)

1885 Safety bike

John Du (1840–1

1817
Karl von Drais builds the dandy horse in Germany

1839
Kirkpatrick Macmillan adds back-wheel pedals to create the pedal bike

1863
Pierre Lallement attaches pedals to the front wheel to create the velocipede

1870
James Starley invent the Ordinary, or Penny Farthing, bike

1839 Pedal bike

Kirkpatrick Macmillan (1812–1878)

1863 Velocipede

1870 Penny Farthing

1992 Olympic superbike

Faster! Faster!

1888 Dunlop tires

1970s BMX

1885
John Kemp Starley invents the Safety bike

1888
John Dunlop invents the air-filled rubber tire

1970s
Small BMX bikes are developed for racing over rugged courses

1992
Great Britain's Chris Boardman wins an Olympic gold medal on the Lotus 108 superbike

BIKES

For centuries, transportation relied on animal power; now most vehicles use engine power. But the most efficient way to move is to use human power; pedaling a bike is the best way to turn an energy source into motion. Let's take a look at where bikes came from. It's quite a ride!

← Velocipede or Boneshaker

1817 The dandy horse

Karl von Drais (1785–1851) invented the first bike in Germany. He called it a *Laufmaschine*, meaning "running machine." It had no pedals; riders sat on the saddle and used their legs to push themselves along. It was hard work! There was also a footrest to keep the riders' feet off the ground when they raced downhill. *Laufmaschine* owners went to riding schools to learn how to use their bikes. Most riders were fashionable young men, who were known as dandies. In the USA and Britain, the machines were named "dandy horses."

1839 The pedal bike

Kirkpatrick Macmillan (1812–1878), a Scottish blacksmith, improved the "dandy horse" by adding pedals. The pedals were made using steam engine connecting rods, which, when turned, created a back-and-forth motion that spun the bike wheel. On Macmillan's bike, only the back wheel turned when the pedals were pushed. This was the first pedal bike, and Macmillan pedaled all over the countryside on it. He must have been very fit because riding his bike was very hard work. His design never really caught on.

1863 Boneshaker

It was nearly 20 years before the next bike was designed. In 1863, French inventor Pierre Lallement (1843–1891) added pedals to the front wheel of his bike. No connecting rods were needed, which made the machine easier to ride, but not very comfortable. Lallement called his machine the Velocipede, but most people called it the "Boneshaker." The bike had a wooden wheel with an iron rim; the rider had to lean back to ride it, and they felt every bump in the road.

1870 Penny Farthing

In 1870, Englishman James Starley (1830–1881) invented the Ordinary bike. On this bike, the rider sat above a large front wheel that was about 5 feet tall. The back wheel was much smaller. With every turn a large wheel goes farther than a small one, and so the giant wheel made the Ordinary very fast. The Ordinary is better known as the Penny Farthing. This was because at the time the British penny coin was very large and the farthing (quarter penny) coin was very small.

Pedal bike

Dandy horse →

Penny Farthing →

1885 Safety bike

In 1885, James Starley's nephew, John Kemp Starley (1854–1901), came up with an even better design. He called it the Safety Bicycle. The front and back wheels were the same size and were connected to the pedals with a chain. Does this sound familiar? Bikes today use the same 1885 design.

Early safety bikes were not as fast as the giant Ordinary bikes, so gears were added to change that. Gears are different cogs used by the bike chain. A big cog makes the wheels turn more times as you pedal, which makes you go faster. A small cog makes the wheel turn fewer times but it takes less work to do it, which is good for going uphill.

BMX

Safety bike

1970 BMX

In the 1970s, another type of bicycle was invented: the BMX (which stands for "bicycle motocross"). A BMX is for riding fast over rugged tracks. It has a small but strong frame. Riders do not need to sit down very often as they race and perform tricks, so the saddle is very low down and safely out of the way. BMX started as a fun sport for kids who wanted to copy off-road motorbike racing. Today BMX is even in the Olympics.

Chris Boardman

John Dunlop

1888 Dunlop tires

Riding a bike still wasn't very comfortable. That was, until Scottish inventor John Dunlop (1840–1921) came along. To make his son's tricycle more comfortable he fitted the wheels with rubber tubes filled with air, and in so doing he invented tires. The tires gave the tricycle a much smoother ride, and they also made it faster. The rubber tire was better at gripping the ground too. Professional cyclists found that using Dunlop's tires made it easier for them to win races.

1992 Olympic superbike

In 1992, the British cyclist Chris Boardman competed at the Olympic Games on a futuristic-looking bike, the Lotus 108 superbike. Boardman's bike used new technology to reduce the resistance of the air pushing on him as he raced. The frame was made from carbon fiber, a lightweight but tough material, shaped to slice through the air as fast as possible. He also wore a helmet that looked like it belonged to a superhero. The helmet helped by streamlining his head and shoulders. Boardman's new look worked—he won the gold medal and changed racing bikes forever.

AIRPLANES

1010
Eilmer of Malmesbury conducts one of the first known flight experiments

1849
Sir George Cayley sends a ten-year-old boy up in the first successful glider flight

1889
Otto Lilienthal tests his gliders in front of cheering crowds

1903
The Wright brothers make the first powered airplane flight in history

1927
Charles Lindbergh crosse the Atlantic in the *Spirit St. Louis*

AIRPLANES

The invention of balloons had proved that it was possible to fly, but they couldn't get very high and they didn't go very fast. To do that, inventors would need to build a machine that copied the way birds fly. However, winged aircraft have a big problem: they are very heavy. Luckily, some brave inventors decided to take the leap and find out how to make them work.

1010 The flying monk

One of the first people known to have experimented with flight was a monk named Eilmer from Malmesbury, England. Eilmer climbed to the top of a tall church tower, strapped a set of bat-like wings to his arms and ankles, and jumped into the air! He crash-landed 650 feet in front of the tower. He did not try again—he had broken both his legs in the crash and never walked properly again.

1800s Wings

By the 1800s, many inventors were starting to develop aircraft. English aristocrat Sir George Cayley (1773–1857) discovered that a wing needed a special shape, known as an airfoil, in order to fly. An airfoil is curved at the top and flat underneath; the air rushes around the shape, creating a lift force that pushes the wing up. Sir George never flew himself but used his servants—and their children—to test his unpowered gliders.

In 1890, French inventor Clément Ader (1841–1925) added a steam engine to a large wing, making a plane called the *Éole*. It could fly short distances but was too heavy to get more than 8 inches off the ground.

German inventor Otto Lilienthal (1848–1896) built gliders with different wing shapes to see which were best for steering and soaring. Lilienthal flew the gliders himself and, in 1894, he built a 45-foot hill—the Fliegeberg or Flight Mountain—on the outskirts of Berlin, where he could test his inventions.

1903 Wright *Flyer 1*

The Wright brothers, Orville (1871–1948) and Wilbur (1867–1912), were big fans of Lilienthal. The brothers designed a biplane (a plane with two sets of wings, one on top of the other) with a lightweight gasoline engine that powered two propellers behind the wings. It was the first airplane.

In December 1903, Orville Wright made the first airplane flight in history. It lasted 12 seconds and covered 120 feet at 7 miles per hour. After practice, Wilbur Wright flew 850 feet and was up in the air for one minute! From these small beginnings, the Wright brothers went on to build bigger and better aircraft. By the start of World War I, all major armies had a fleet of planes based on the Wright brothers' model.

The Wright Brothers and *Flyer 1*

1927 Going transatlantic

In 1927, Charles Lindbergh (1902–1974), an American airmail pilot, made history by being the first person to fly solo across the Atlantic Ocean. Lindbergh did it alone in a tiny monoplane called the *Spirit of St. Louis*. The plane was very light, but it contained a huge fuel tank. Lindbergh stayed in the air for 33 hours, dodging storms, fog banks, and big waves as he flew low over the ocean. Navigating by the stars, he found his way from Long Island, New York, to Paris, France, and was met by a huge crowd. Overnight he had become the most famous flyer in the world.

Spirit of St. Louis

1947 Bell X-1

In October 1947, Chuck Yeager (born 1923), a tough US pilot, took control of the Bell X-1, a little bullet-shaped plane powered by a rocket engine. It had to be dropped from a B-29 to start its flight and was built to fly at a supersonic speed, punching through the sound barrier (a mass of tightly squeezed air that builds up in front of the plane as it speeds up). It made a thundering sound as it rushed through the sky—this is known as the sonic boom.

Bell X-1

1944 Jet aircraft

World War II saw advances in aircraft technology. In 1944, a new sound filled the skies—the deep roar of a jet engine. A jet aircraft used a blast of hot gases to push through the air, meaning it could fly higher and faster than propeller planes. The first jet aircraft to be made in large numbers was the German Me 262. It could reach 540 miles per hour, which was almost one and a half times as fast as rival propeller planes.

Spruce Goose

1947 *Spruce Goose*

Howard Hughes (1905–1976), an eccentric US millionaire businessman, took the controls of the Hercules H-4, later nicknamed *Spruce Goose*. This giant flying boat was designed to take off and land on water. It was made from wood, had eight propeller engines, and had the biggest wings of any plane in history. Hughes flew the monster plane just one mile to show it worked—it has never flown anywhere since!

Me 262 fighter

TANKS

The roughest, toughest vehicles around are tanks. Tanks are military machines and are built to protect the soldiers inside. They are basically like mobile castles, and the very first ones were built as anti-castle attack weapons.

Motor Scout

305 BCE Helepolis Tower

The first armored vehicle was also the largest ever built. In 305 BCE, the ancient Greek army laid siege to the city of Rhodes using a machine called the Helepolis Tower. It was 130 feet high, with nine stories, and was made from wood. The back of the tower was open, but the rest of it was covered in iron plates to protect the soldiers inside from arrows and fire. Inside, soldiers fired ammunition from catapults through hatches in the front. However, the attack failed. The defenders poured mud, water, and sewage in front of the wheels so the machine got stuck.

Helepolis Tower →

1898 Motor Scout

The first car built for the battlefield was the Motor Scout, designed by British engineer Frederick Simms (1863–1944). This machine did not look very safe. It was a four-wheel quad bike with a small motor and a machine gun attached.

The following year, Simms built the Motor War Car, which looked like a giant upside-down bathtub. It had more protection than the Motor Scout, but the driver still had to stand up to look over the top at the enemy. Generals never sent the Motor War Car into battle and continued to look for a better fighting machine.

Motor War Car

1400s CE Wagon fortress

Ever since they were first invented, wagons were popular battle vehicles. However, they were very slow. In the 15th century, the Hussite army from central Europe improved the war wagon. These wagons had high walls made from thick wood, and archers fired at the enemy through a small opening in the side. In big battles, hundreds of war wagons lined up to make a "wagon fortress."

1487 Leonardo da Vinci's tank

In 1487, the Italian artist and engineer Leonardo da Vinci (1452–1519) (who is most famous for painting the *Mona Lisa*) sketched a design for the first tank. It was wooden, armored with metal plates, and had a cone-shaped roof. (The idea was that arrows and cannonballs would bounce off the slanted sides.) This invention would never have worked—on soft ground, it would have been too heavy to move.

The Hussite army wagon →

Leonardo da Vinci tank →

Leonardo da Vinci ↑

1916 Mark I

In 1916, the British Army used a new weapon. It was officially named the Mark I, but everyone called it the tank. The Mark I was a metal box with a slanted shape. The British Army wanted to keep its true purpose secret while it was being built, so they pretended it was a storage tank, and the name has stuck ever since. The Mark I did not run on wheels; it used caterpillar tracks that ran around the outside, which were better at gripping the ground. The machine's slanted shape meant that the tracks were always in contact with the ground, so the tank could roll through holes and over trenches. A crew of eight could fit inside and fire guns at the enemy. The age of the tank had arrived.

Mark I

1943 Tank battle

By World War II, tanks were faster and had even better armor. In 1943, one of the biggest tank battles in history took place in Kursk, in the Soviet Union. Eight thousand tanks from the Soviet Union and Germany went head to head. The German tanks lost, and from then on the Germans began to retreat all over Europe.

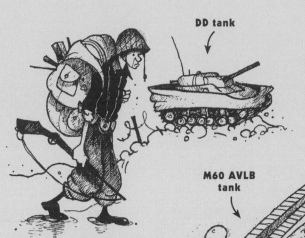

DD tank

1944 D-Day

In 1944, the World War II battle known as the Normandy landings, or D-Day, took place. US, British, and Canadian soldiers landed in France using DD tanks—this is short for Duplex Drive but they were nicknamed "Donald Duck." These tanks had a watertight bag around the outside, so they could float. They drove their ships into the water and sailed to the shore. Once on dry land, the crew switched power to the tracks and drove into battle.

1960 M60 AVLB

The US Army's M60 AVLB is a tank with a difference. The name stands for Armored Vehicle-Launched Bridge. A 60-foot bridge, with a hinge in the middle, is folded up on top of the tank. The bridge can be unfolded and placed over a small river or big hole in a road. Then other vehicles can cross.

M60 AVLB tank

2002 Personnel carrier

Tanks are less common in modern armies because they are vulnerable to attack from the air. Modern armies use smaller, more nimble armored fighting vehicles, such as the Stryker. They carry a small force of soldiers into battle; the vehicle's thick armor and big gun protect the soldiers from attack until it is safe to leave the vehicle. These vehicles have thick tires instead of caterpillar tracks. Each wheel is turned by the engine, so if one wheel is damaged the vehicle can keep going. All the wheels can turn to face different directions so the big vehicle can turn around very quickly.

The Stryker

Tank battle

HELICOPTERS

1480
Aerial Screw

1923
Autogyro

Aha! I know that it can go up now, but how will it stay there?

1877
Steam hover

Enrico Forlanini
(1848–1930)

400 BCE
First helicopter

Leonardo da Vinci
(1452–1519)

2000
V-22
Osprey

1480s
Leonardo da Vinci sketches a design for an Aerial Screw, a helicopter that used a spiral sail

1877
Enrico Forlanini tries out an uncrewed model helicopter powered by a steam engine

1923
Juan de la Cierva invents the autogyro, an aircraft that is halfway between an airplane and a helicopter

1939
Igor Sikorsky builds the first fully functioning helicopter

1939
First actual
helicopter

Igor Sikorsky
(1889–1972)

I've made a helicopter that can go in any direction —even backward!

1962
Skycrane

1968
The Russian
Mil V-12

2005
Didier
Delsalle

1962
The Skycrane, a heavy lifting helicopter design, is used to transport cargo during battles and emergencies

1968
The Russian Mil V-12, the biggest helicopter ever, is built

2000
The V-22 Osprey is introduced by the US Marines. It can fly like an airplane or a helicopter

2005
Didier Delsalle is the first pilot to land on the summit of Mount Everest and take off again

HELICOPTERS

An airplane can go anywhere—up, down, and all over the world. But when it wants to take off or land, it needs a wide flat area—an airport, for example. A helicopter does not have this problem. It can fly straight up off the ground, and then go straight back down again. And if the pilot just wants to stop, a helicopter can hover in mid-air!

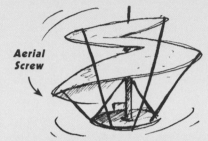

Aerial Screw

1480s *Aerial Screw*

The first helicopter was made by a Chinese toymaker. The toy had a string that, when pulled, made pieces of bamboo spin around very fast and then fly up into the air. The first person to consider using a helicopter as a machine people could fly in was Leonardo da Vinci (1452–1519). In the early 1480s, he sketched the *Aerial Screw*, which had a spiral-shaped sail around a pole. Da Vinci claimed that spinning the sail would pull the aircraft upward in the same way a metal screw pulls itself into wood. It was a good idea, but it would be too heavy to actually work.

Gyroplane

1923 Gyroplane

In 1923, a Spanish aviator called Juan de la Cierva (1895–1936) took to the air in a rather strange-looking aircraft. It had a propeller at the front but no wings. Instead it had a rotor made of four wing-shaped blades, which spun around. De la Cierva called his aircraft a gyroplane, but it is also known as an autogyro. As he sped down the runway, the air made the rotor turn very fast. This is called autorotation, and it makes the rotor lift the aircraft like the wing of a normal airplane. Autogyros were popular in the 1930s, but they were harder to use than planes and did not do anything special.

1939 The first helicopter

Rotors and wings both create lift so an aircraft can fly. When an airplane turns on its engine and races down the runway, the air passing under and over the wing lifts the airplane forward into the sky. In a helicopter, the engine turns the rotor and makes enough lift to pull the aircraft straight up into the air.

In 1939, the Russian-American inventor Igor Sikorsky (1889–1972) figured out how to control the lift of the rotor so the helicopter could take off, land, and fly in any direction—even backward. He added a series of hinges to each rotor blade, which made them twist in different directions as the rotor spun. By controlling the position of each blade, Sikorsky could steer the helicopter. If he balanced the weight and lift perfectly, the helicopter just hovered in midair.

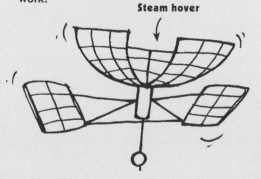

Steam hover

1877 Steam hover

In 1877, the Italian inventor Enrico Forlanini (1848–1930) built a model helicopter inspired by Leonardo's sketch. It had a rotor, or rotating wing, made from wood and sailcloth and was spun by a steam engine. Forlanini tested the machine in his local park in Milan. It reached a height of 40 feet, but only stayed in the air for 20 seconds. Forlanini had proved that helicopters could fly upwards; he hadn't figured out how to make it stay in the air.

The first actual helicopter

Skycrane

2000 V-22 Osprey

In 2000, a new kind of helicopter was revealed. The V-22 Osprey is a tiltrotor. Like the Mil V-12, it has two big rotors on either side of a large cabin. The Osprey can take off straight up into the air, but once in the air, it tilts the rotors so they face forward, and it starts flying like an airplane. When the Osprey arrives at its destination, it tilts its rotor upward again and just hovers on the spot.

V-22 Osprey

1962 Skycrane

Sikorsky was the leading helicopter developer in the world. In 1962, his company produced the Skycrane. This giant helicopter had a cockpit for crew but carried cargo externally. The Skycrane could lift enormous loads, including houses, other helicopters, tanks, and almost anything that weighed up to 13 tons.

Russian Mil V-12

2005 Helicopter rescue

Helicopters cannot fly as high as airplanes. The air gets thinner the higher up you go, and it doesn't provide enough lift around the rotors. In 2005, Frenchman Didier Delsalle managed to fly all the way to the top of Mount Everest, which is over 29,000 feet high. To get there, he had to ride on the winds that were blowing up the mountain. He landed on the top and then took off again. He used a small helicopter, with nothing in the cabin but his seat, so the aircraft was as light as possible. Not only did Delsalle break a world record, he also rescued two climbers who had gotten hurt halfway down the mountain.

Helicopter rescue

1968 Mil V-12

The biggest helicopter ever built was the Mil V-12, invented in Russia. It looked a lot like a passenger jet and even had seats for 196 people. Out of each side it had supports for two immense rotors. Each rotor had four blades, and each blade was almost as long as a tennis court. Only two Mil V-12s were ever built in 1968. They could lift 44 tons— which is equivalent to 90 polar bears!

WORKING VEHICLES

1860
Traction
engine

1730
Newsham
fire
engine

Early 19th century
omnibus

1882
Trolley bus

1908
Double-decker
bus

1721
Richard Newsham
invents the first fire engine

1860
Thomas Aveling invents
the traction engine

1908
The X-Type, the first double-
decker bus, starts carrying
passengers in London

1914
The Holt 120 tractor was
designed with caterpillar
tracks like a tank

1995
Bagger 293

1914
Holt 120 tractor

2014
The BelAZ
75710

1923
Snowplow

1940 Army general
purpose vehicle
(jeep)

1930
Australian
road train

1930
The first road trains start running
in Australia, becoming the largest
road vehicles in the world

1940
General Purpose (GP) vehicles
are introduced for the US Army

1995
A giant digger called Bagger
293, the largest wheeled vehicle
in history, begins working at
coal mines in Germany

2014
The BelAZ 75710 tipper truck
becomes the largest in the world,
able to carry 500 tons at once

WORKING VEHICLES

Working vehicles are tough and strong, built to lift and shift whatever we need. Some we see every day, others are less common, and some of these motorized monsters are bigger than a house—and they have very big jobs to do.

Traction engine

1860 Traction engine

By the 1850s, steam engines had replaced human workers on the majority of farms in western Europe. But it was difficult to get big steam engines to where they were needed.

So Thomas Aveling (1824–1882) invented the traction engine—a steam engine that could be driven to where it needed to work. It could pull plows, run pumps, drive threshing machines (for getting the wheat grains off the straw stalks), and also pull the farmer's wagon. Early traction engines had huge wheels taller than a person and were very slow. Farmers started using smaller traction engines that became known simply as tractors.

Newsham fire engine

1721 Fire engine

Until the 19th century, most houses in cities were built from wood, and when one caught fire the whole neighborhood would go up in flames. Fire brigades rushed to put the fire out, using buckets of water carried from local rivers. In 1730, Richard Newsham (d. 1743), an English inventor, introduced the fire engine in Philadelphia. It was a horse-drawn wagon with a water tank. Once the wagon had been hauled to the fire, firefighters would pump the water out by hand. The tank contained 170 gallons of water, which could be pumped onto a fire in less than two minutes. Fire engines are a lot more powerful now.

1800s Buses

The word "bus" comes from the Latin word "omnibus," which means "for all." The first omnibuses were large horse-drawn wagons used in the early 19th century. Inventors came up with all kinds of ways to improve the omnibus. Steam engines were added, but these puffing monsters were only allowed to go two miles per hour! The trolleybus had an electric motor, powered by wires hanging overhead. When the wires ran out, the bus stopped. The best buses were powered by diesel engines. In 1908, a second floor was added to some buses, creating a double-decker. The first double-decker was the X type and was used in London.

Early 19th century omnibus

Double decker b

Bagger 293

Snowplow

Army general purpose vehicle (jeep)

1995 Monster digger

The biggest-wheeled vehicle ever made is Bagger 293. Completed in 1995, this huge vehicle scrapes coal from the ground in a German mine. It is 300 feet tall and over 700 feet long, weighs 15,000 tons, and has a four-billion horsepower engine—that makes it four million times more powerful than the best racing car! Bagger could scoop up an entire Olympic swimming pool of water in its massive shovels in just two minutes. It can move using 12 caterpillar tracks, although it's very slow—at top speed it takes 10 minutes to go 300 feet!

1923 Snowplow

The snowplow was invented around the same time as the bulldozer, and it works in the same kind of way. The difference is that the blade is pointed, so it cuts into the snow and pushes it to the side, not straight ahead like a bulldozer.

1930 Road train

A road train is a big truck that pulls four trailers. Australian road trains weigh more than 200 tons, which is about the same as 50 killer whales. They run on long, straight roads through the desert and have a top speed of 60 miles per hour.

1940 General Purpose

A four-wheel-drive car has an engine that powers all four of its wheels, whereas the engine of a normal car only powers the front two. Four-wheel drive helps the vehicle move over rough ground where there are no roads. If one or two wheels cannot grip the ground, the others will still be able to push the car along. One of the first off-road four-wheel cars was the General Purpose vehicle, or GP, which was used by the US military in World War II. The American soldiers preferred to call it the "jeep," which is what we call most off-road cars today.

The BelAZ 75710

2014 Tipper truck

The biggest tipper truck, the BelAZ 75710, was built by a Belorussian company in 2014. Each tire is over 6 feet tall, and the truck can carry 500 tons—that's the weight of ten houses. The truck is as tall as a house as well. The driver has to climb up a flight of stairs to get to the driver's seat!

Australian road train

SUBMARINES

David Bushnell
(1740–1824)

1775
Bushnell
Turtle

1620
Drebbel
submarine

330s BCE
Diving bell

1964
Alvin submarine

1960
Trieste
submarine

330s BCE
Alexander the Great is said
to have used a diving bell
to explore underwater

1620 CE
Cornelis Drebbel launches
the first submarine in the
River Thames

1775
David Bushnell builds the
Turtle to attack British ships
in the American Revolution

1800
Robert Fulton builds
the *Nautilus,* the first
submarine

1800
Fulton *Nautilus*

1954
USS *Nautilus*

2012
First solo dive
into the Mariana
Trench

1912
Titanic
wreck

1939
The British Navy reveals
they use sonar for
detecting submarines

1958
The nuclear-powered USS
Nautilus sails underwater
to the North Pole

1960
The *Trieste* submarine
reaches the bottom of the
Mariana Trench

1986
The submersible *Alvin* visits
the wreck of the *Titanic*

2012
James Cameron makes
the first solo dive into the
Mariana Trench

SUBMARINES

Most people crisscross the land by car, bus, and train. However, only a small percent of the places to go on earth are actually above land. The rest are under water. We almost never go under the sea, and there are many things still to discover. To visit the deep we need a very special vehicle, something that can sink but still float—a submarine.

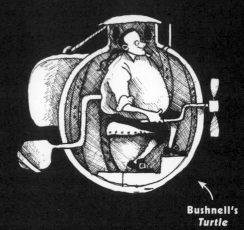

Bushnell's *Turtle*

Diving bell

1620 Drebbel submarine

It is said that King James I of England (1566–1625) took a ride in the world's first actual submarine, built by a Dutch inventor, Cornelis Drebbel (1572–1633).

The wooden Drebbel submarine was a bit like a rowboat with curved sides that met at the top. It was powered and steered by oars covered by leather sleeves that stuck out of holes.

Some reports claim Drebbel's submarine took a three-hour dive in the River Thames and traveled 15 feet under the surface. Most modern experts think it probably just sat on the bottom of the river or was pulled along by the current. No one knows for sure. Drebbel often made up stories about his machines!

1775 *Turtle*

The next submarine was the *Turtle*, a one-person attack boat built by American David Bushnell (1740–1824). Bushnell's craft was designed to sink British ships during the American Revolutionary War (1775–1783). It was a sealed wooden barrel that had a little tower made from metal and glass on top so Bushnell could look around. The *Turtle* had two propellers: one was used to drive backward and forward and the other was used to make the submarine go up and down—the enemy would never see it coming underwater.

330s BCE Diving bell

The ancient Greek emperor Alexander the Great (356–323 BCE) is one of the earliest recorded underwater explorers. About 2,300 years ago he traveled down into the sea inside a diving bell. This was a bell-shaped vessel that was lowered into the water; the air inside stopped the water coming in—like an upside-down cup in the bath.

Drebbel submarine

Fulton's *Nautilus*

1800 *Nautilus*

In 1800, American Robert Fulton (1765–1815) built a submarine that actually worked! It was called the *Nautilus* and was built to sink enemy warships. The *Nautilus* had room for four crew members. It had tanks that flooded to make the craft sink. Once underwater, the crew cranked a large propeller to push the boat along. To surface again, the crew pumped the water out of the tanks, and up they went.

1939 Sonar

The *Nautilus* was designed for war and it carried a self-propelled underwater bomb. Fulton called the bomb a "torpedo" (after the fish that gives nasty electric shocks). In World War I, submarines were used in battle for the first time and their torpedoes were a major threat to warships. In response, the British navy invented the ASDIC machine (meaning Anti-Submarine Detector). The ASDIC sent a *ping* sound into the water underneath ships; if there was a submarine down there, the ping echoed back to alert the crew. ASDIC is now known as sonar.

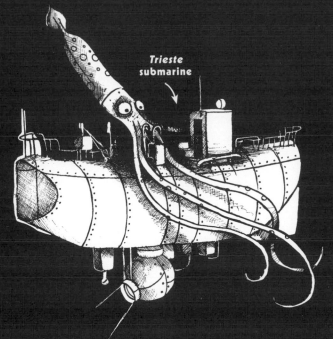

Trieste submarine

1960 *Trieste*

Even the best military submarines rarely go deeper than 2000 feet underwater. In 1960, a crew of two, Jacques Piccard (1922–2008) from Switzerland and Don Walsh (b. 1931) from America, went 18 times deeper in a submarine called the *Trieste*. They ventured to the bottom of the Mariana Trench, which at nearly seven miles below sea level is the deepest place on Earth. If you put Mount Everest into the trench, its summit would still be a mile below the surface! The *Trieste* is a thick metal ball that sits under a heavy tank of gasoline; it took nearly five hours for heavy weights to pull the *Trieste* down to the bottom. The pressure at the bottom is 1,000 times stronger than at the surface. (This caused one of the windows to crack, but luckily it didn't break.)

1954 *Nautilus*

In 1954, the United States Navy launched a new submarine called the *Nautilus*. It may have had the same name as Fulton's early model but it could not have been more different! Instead of turning the propeller by hand, the USS *Nautilus* was powered by a nuclear reactor. It could make its own air by splitting water to release oxygen gas, and it had enough fuel on board to last years. In 1958, the *Nautilus* sailed under the ice all the way to the North Pole.

USS Nautilus

Alvin submarine

1986 *Alvin* visits *Titanic*

Submarines that take explorers into deep water are called submersibles. In 1986, sonar detectors hung from a surface ship discovered the wreck of the *Titanic* lying nearly three miles underwater in the North Atlantic. The following year a submersible called *Alvin* was sent down to take a closer look. The crew of *Alvin* used a small robot submarine called *Jason Junior* to video the wreck.

Titanic wreck

ROCKETS

1600
Wan Hu's
rocket chair

1944
V-2 rocket
bomb

1957 Sputnik 1
satellite

Konstantin
Tsiolkovsky
(1857–1935)

1967
Soyuz
Spacecraft

1600s
Wan Hu tries to use
fireworks to reach space
and is never seen again

1903
Konstantin Tsiolkovsky
proposes the idea of a
rocket train

1944
On a test flight, the V-2
rocket bomb becomes
the first vehicle to
enter space

1957
Sputnik 1 is the first spacecraft to
orbit earth. A few months later,
Laika the dog becomes the first
animal to orbit earth

1969
Apollo 11

Laika

1969
Moonwalk (Buzz Aldrin, Neil Armstrong)

Yuri Gagarin
(1934–1968)

1990
Hubble telescope

1981
Space shuttle
Columbia

2004
SpaceShipOne

1961
Russian pilot Yuri Gagarin is the first person to travel into space and orbit earth

1967
The Russian Soyuz spacecraft begins taking astronauts into orbit

1969
The Saturn V rocket blasts the crew of Apollo 11 to the Moon

1981
Space shuttle *Columbia*, the first reusable spacecraft, goes into service

2004
SpaceShipOne is the first vehicle to fly into space twice in two weeks

ROCKETS

Rockets are the most powerful engines that have ever been built. They are powerful enough to blast people into space to send them to the Moon and maybe even to other planets. Rockets are actually the oldest type of engine ever invented.

V2 rocket bomb

Around 1040 CE Rocket power

The first rocket engines were invented in China and were basically fireworks fueled by gunpowder. When set alight, the chemicals in gunpowder react so fast that they explode into hot gases. A firework directs these hot gases out the bottom, and the blast of gas pushes the rocket up. Rockets that go to space work like this too, but they go off with a bigger bang.

1500 The first astronaut?

According to a Chinese story, Wan Hu was the first spaceman. He tied 47 large gunpowder rockets to his chair, sat down, and ordered 47 helpers to light every rocket at the same time. Next there came a roaring whoosh of flames and smoke. When the air cleared, Wan Hu and his chair had disappeared. He was never seen again. Did he get to space?

Wan Hu

1903 Rocket man

Many 19th-century writers and scientists suggested that humans could visit space. In 1903, Russian mathematics teacher Konstantin Tsiolkovsky (1857–1935) figured out that getting into space would only be possible by using rocket engines. He showed how to calculate the size rocket needed to carry different loads into orbit. Space scientists still use his calculation today. Tsiolkovsky also invented the "rocket train"—a rocket built from several stages that take turns pushing a heavy spacecraft into orbit. This is exactly how rockets are built today. The first stage at the bottom of the rocket launches the spacecraft. When it runs out of fuel, the heavy first stage falls away, and a second stage takes over to push the craft into space.

Konstantin Tsiolkovsky

1944 V2 rocket bomb

In World War II, German engineers built the V2 rocket powered by liquid fuels. In a 1944 test flight, a V2 flew for more than 118 miles 50 miles up; it was the first vehicle to ever fly into space. However, the V2 was not built as a spacecraft but as a flying bomb to attack enemy cities.

Between 1948 and 1949, American rocket engineers launched monkeys into space inside four unused V2s they had captured from Germany (with the bomb removed). For some reason the cute passengers were all called Albert. Only Albert II reached space, but sadly he died when his space capsule crash-landed.

1957 Russians reach space

After World War II, rocket scientists in America and Russia raced each other to build bigger, faster, and more powerful rockets, mostly for making terrifying bombs. However, they were also developing spacecraft. The Russian scientists won the race in 1957 when they launched the first satellite, Sputnik 1. This shiny sphere could be seen with telescopes and gave out a radio signal.

A few months later they launched Sputnik 2, which had a passenger—a dog named Laika. She became the first animal to orbit Earth, but she never came home. In 1961, Yuri Gagarin (1934–1968), a Russian pilot, became the first human to fly into space and orbit Earth. He did come home, hurtling back through the atmosphere in a round capsule that parachuted into the desert of Central Asia.

Laika

Sputnik 1 →

1969 Moon walk

In July 1969, US astronaut Neil Armstrong (1930–2012) became the first human to walk on the Moon—soon followed by his crewmate Buzz Aldrin (b. 1930).

The mission to the Moon was called the Apollo program. It used the tallest vehicle in history, the Saturn V rocket—it was 60 feet taller than the Statue of Liberty! The Saturn V launch in Florida made the loudest artificial sound ever and its engine was millions of times more powerful than a jumbo jet's during taking off. The roar of the engines was so loud they made the ground shake (only a tiny bit though) as far away as New York.

Only 12 people have visited the Moon. The last person on the Moon was Eugene Cernan (1934–2017); he left his footprints there in December 1972. No one has been back since.

Space shuttle

1981 Space shuttle

Using Saturn Vs to blast people into space was enormously expensive. So NASA (the American space agency) built a cheaper, reusable spacecraft that could fly into space like a rocket but could glide back home like an airplane. NASA called it the Space Transportation System (also known as the space shuttle). In total, five space shuttles were built. Starting in 1981, with the space shuttle *Columbia*, the shuttles made 135 missions into space, launching famous satellites like the Hubble Space Telescope and sections of the International Space Station, which were then connected together in space. The shuttles were grounded in 2011 because it became too expensive to launch them safely.

2004 SpaceShipOne

SpaceShipOne was the first vehicle to fly into space twice in two weeks. It was carried into the air by a jet-powered mothership and then blasted off to the edge of space, before gliding back to land. A larger model, SpaceShipTwo, is currently being built to carry tourists on spaceflights.

Space flight today and tomorrow

The safest way to get into space—and back again—is in a three-person Soyuz spacecraft. These are launched from Baikonur, a spaceport in Kazakhstan. Since 1967, more than 130 Soyuz spacecraft have launched hundreds of astronauts from more than 30 countries into space.

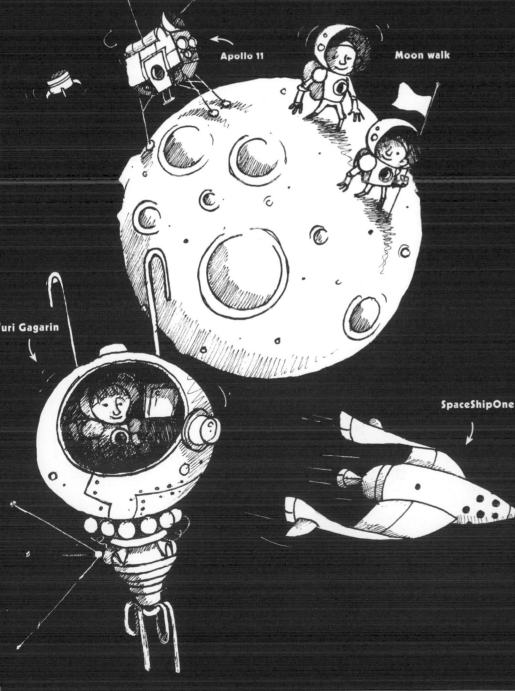

Apollo 11 →   Moon walk

uri Gagarin

SpaceShipOne ↓

SPACECRAFT

1962
Mariner 2

1971
The first
space station
Salyut

1977
The Voyager
probe

Saturn

1972
Venera 8

Venus

Pluto

2015
New Horizons
probe

1959
Luna 2, a Russian
space probe, crash-
lands on the Moon

1962
Mariner 2, an
American spacecraft,
makes the first fly-by
of Venus

1966
Luna 9 makes the
first soft landing
on the surface of
the Moon

1970
Lunokhod 1 lands
on the Moon and is
the first rover to visit
another world

1971
The Russian space
agency launches the
first space station.

SPACECRAFT

If you could fly into space, where would you want to go? Over the last 60 years, engineers have figured out ways to travel to the Moon, other planets, and even to tiny comets. To get there they have invented a range of spacecraft that use airbags, cranes, rockets, and even a space slingshot.

Lunokhod 1 rover

1959 Shooting the Moon

The first spacecraft to reach the Moon was the Russian robotic probe Luna 2 in 1959. It did not orbit Earth; the shiny, round spacecraft flew straight to the Moon. Then it smashed right into it! This sounds clumsy, but it was actually the plan all along. A crash landing was much easier to do than a controlled, or soft, landing and it told scientists a lot about what the Moon was made of.

In 2005, a different kind of crash landing was arranged for the comet Tempel. A Deep Impact space probe fired a camera at the comet. The camera kept on snapping pictures right up until it crashed. The crash made a crater in the comet's surface which gave the Deep Impact probe a good view of what the comet was made of.

Luna 2 robotic probe

1970 Taking a ride on the Moon

In 1970, Russia sent the Lunokhod 1 rover to have a drive around. Lunokhod 1 looked like a bath riding on eight wheels. It was a robot that was controlled by scientists on Earth, using solar power during the day (when the sun was shining on the Moon) and kept warm at night because it had a radioactive heater deep inside. Lunokhod 1 drove 6 miles on the Moon in just under a year.

1962 Flying visits to other planets

The first probe to visit another planet was Mariner 2. In 1962, Mariner 2 flew 21,600 miles above the surface of Venus taking pictures, measuring the planet's temperature, and scanning the planet with radio waves. Mariner 2 revealed that Venus was covered in thick white clouds. These clouds make Venus shine brightly in the sky, but they also block out any view of the planet's surface underneath.

In 2015, the New Horizons probe made a fly-by of Pluto. Pluto is more than 100 times farther away from Earth than Venus is, and it took nine years to fly there.

1966 Touch down on the Moon

In 1966, the Russian probe Luna 9 was the first space probe to make a soft landing on the moon and survive. On its way down, Luna 9 inflated a big airbag to cushion its fall. This also meant it bounced around on the Moon for while, before coming to a stop.

Luna 9

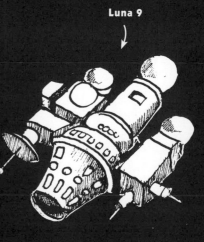

Mariner 2

1971 Orbiting other planets

In 1971, Mariner 9 became the first spacecraft to orbit another planet—Mars. To do that, it had to follow an exact path through space at an exact speed. If it went too slow it would crash, and if it went too fast it would fly straight past. The spacecraft went into orbit around Mars for more than a year and sent back pictures of the surface. It saw dust storms that covered the whole planet, discovered the Solar System's largest mountain, called Olympus Mons, and a huge canyon, called Valles Marineris, that is wide enough to fit the whole of the United States inside!

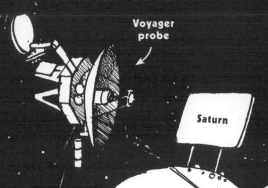

Voyager probe

Saturn

1977 Slingshot

Voyager probes were big spacecraft that were sent on a grand tour of the outer planets, from Jupiter to Neptune. They discovered all kinds of things: Jupiter's ice moons, Uranus's rings, and the fastest winds ever measured on Neptune (they whirled ten times faster than a tornado). To make the journey, they used a system called a gravity assist. The spacecraft zoomed in at high speed behind each planet. Once it got close to the planet, the planet's gravity pulled on the Voyager, making it speed up and curve around the planet. But the spacecraft was going too fast to get stuck in orbit, so it was flung out the other side—heading toward its next destination, and going even faster. The Voyagers can't come back to Earth, they just keep whizzing deeper into space. They still send messages home every few months to tell us what it's like up there.

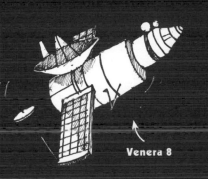

Venera 8

Viking 1

1972 Going interplanetary

Venera 8, a Russian lander, made it to the surface of Venus in 1972. The climate of Venus is hotter than an oven and its air is 90 times thicker than Earth's (and filled with acid), so Venera broke down in less than an hour.

NASA's Viking 1 made the first successful Mars landing in 1976. It took the first color photographs of Mars. They were supposed to check the colors in the photographs against the red, white, and blue American flag on the spacecraft to figure out the true colors of Mars's rocks. But something went wrong; they thought Mars's sky must be blue, which made the red planet's rocks appear green. In the end they realized that the sky was actually turned pink by dust that made the planet look different colors.

The best pictures of Mars were taken in 2012 by the Curiosity rover, a robot explorer. Curiosity used a new kind of landing system—a combination of rockets and a parachute slowed it down as it fell toward the surface. When it was 60 feet above the surface, a rocket-powered "sky crane" took over. This hovered above the planet and lowered the rover gently to the ground.

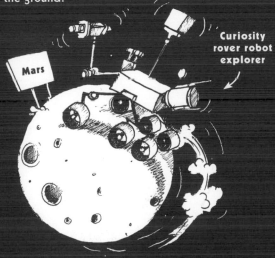

Mars

Curiosity rover robot explorer

2000 A home in space

In 1971, the Russian space agency launched the first space station, Salyut 1. Until 2000, crews only stayed in space stations for a few weeks or months. Then the International Space Station was built. It is big enough to see from Earth (if you know where to look), it weighs nearly 450 tons and would only just fit inside a football stadium. Since 2000, there has been a crew of at least two astronauts on board the ISS at all times. The crew gets fresh food from automatic supply ships sent from Earth.

The ISS is the first permanent home in space. Where will we go to live next? The Moon? Mars? Watch this space.

For Ned, Martha, and Edie —T. J.

For Frances Andrews, who encouraged me to draw when I was feeling lost
and alone in the world. With love and thanks. —C. M.

BLOOMSBURY CHILDREN'S BOOKS
Bloomsbury Publishing Inc., part of Bloomsbury Publishing Plc
1385 Broadway, New York, NY 10018

BLOOMSBURY, BLOOMSBURY CHILDREN'S BOOKS, and the Diana logo
are trademarks of Bloomsbury Publishing Plc

First published in Great Britain as *Amazing Transport* in February 2019 by Bloomsbury Publishing Plc
Published in the United States of America in January 2020
by Bloomsbury Children's Books

Text copyright © 2019 by Tom Jackson
Illustrations copyright © 2019 by Chris Mould

Bloomsbury books may be purchased for business or promotional use. For information on bulk purchases
please contact Macmillan Corporate and Premium Sales Department at specialmarkets@macmillan.com

Library of Congress Cataloging-in-Publication Data
Names: Jackson, Tom, author. | Mould, Chris, illustrator.
Title: Machines in motion : the amazing history of transportation /
by Tom Jackson ; illustrated by Chris Mould.
Description: New York : Bloomsbury, 2020.
Identifiers: LCCN 2019020662 (print)
ISBN 978-1-5476-0337-4 (hardcover)
ISBN 978-1-5476-0338-1 (e-book) • ISBN 978-1-5476-0339-8 (e-PDF)
Subjects: LCSH: Transportation—History—Juvenile literature.
Classification: LCC HE152 .J28 2020 (print) | LCC HE152 (e-book) | DDC 388.09—dc23
LC record available at https://lccn.loc.gov/2019020662
LC e-book record available at https://lccn.loc.gov/2019981470

Printed and bound in China by Leo Paper Products, Heshan, Guangdong
2 4 6 8 10 9 7 5 3 1

All papers used by Bloomsbury Publishing Plc are natural, recyclable products made from wood grown in
well-managed forests. The manufacturing processes conform to the environmental regulations of the country of origin.

To find out more about our authors and books visit www.bloomsbury.com and sign up for our newsletters.